the OPERA of PEACE

For Rayph,
who knows his lines.

the
Opera
of Peace

Flowing in the Trenches, Book 2

REBEKAH TELLER

CONTENTS

Noise

I'm drowsy
In these noisy sounds.
I cannot snooze.
I'm down to
Laying loose.
Without a doubt,
I'm hopeless about
Passing out.

All I can think is
To complain
About these noisy sounds
That drain
My restless mind
After a day
Of messing up
In lots of ways.

I call out to my mom and say,
"I'll never snooze again this way.
How can I sleep
With all these heaps
Of oozing
Drowning out relief?
I'm only losing
So much sleep."

She leans into my door and says,
"There's one thing you can do to rest.
Open your ears to understand

Cicadas are not from your land.
The noise they make is not for us.
They play their very own chorus.
So close your eyes and fall asleep
And find the melody they seek.
To still your mind,
Unwind
And let their kind
Play out their own sweet beat."

Froggy

My mom acts like a busy bee,
But really she's a frog you see.
She likes to hop around the trees
And shudders when there's too much breeze.

When hungry flies circle about,
Her stretchy tongue comes reaching out
To pull those flies into her house
And take them in without a doubt.

She loves to sit upon a log,
But slips away from slobbery dogs
Because she's not sure where they stand
And fears a bite upon her hand.

She tries to stay out in the sun,
And she can have a little fun.
But in a while, she is done
And thinks the heat is for no one.

And though she chirps into the light,
She really likes to sing at night
With stars and fireflies in sight
That glow beneath the moon so bright.

And when the night is done, she goes
Inside her soft and mossy robe
To close her eyes and sink her toes
Into a foamy bed she knows.

Wish

My sister Plan, she likes to swish
And dance and sway
And make a wish.
So I think she's a speedy fish
Who swiftly slips
Through every list.
She doesn't want to hop or stop.
Doesn't want to stand or drop.
She glides along with a big school
And likes when waves are long and cool.

When I look really closely, though,
I think she wants a bigger show.
I think a dolphin's what she is
Instead of any smallish fish.
She wants some time to show her stuff,
Wants to be more than enough,
And leap up high
Toward the sky
Then dive
Back to her swishy jive.

So maybe someday she will see
She's really a dolphin to me,
And all her lists and waves and sand
Are just part of a bigger Plan.

Sticky

The youngest sister of we three,
She really is a busy bee.
She loves to buzz around and see
What all the flowers say or need.

Her hive is stacked with shelves
That smack of sweet reminders
Sticking fast
And cubbies full
Of honeycomb
For all the bees
who come home soon.

The problem for a busy bee
Is honey's pretty darn sticky
And even though they need the hive
They long to freely buzz and fly.

Sometimes I wonder about Bliss
And all the flowers she might miss.
I hope she gets to do her thing
And no one has to feel her sting.

Rainy Day

We were in Mississip
On a hot summer trip,
Camping in an RV,
Near some trees by the sea.

By the ocean we played
In the sand and the waves
'Til this one rainy day
Said inside we should stay.

My dad rolled his eyes,
And mom huffed while he sighed.
Then our neighbor said, "Hey,
Don't let rain waste your day.
There's a place that I know,
You could go to the show.
There's a movie nearby
And you'd have a good time."

Momma thought that show almost sounded fine.

She said, "Well I think
Little Bliss would just sleep,
And Plan here likes to see
A big bright new movie.
But Bekah's at an age
That's a wiggly stage
And she wouldn't hold still
For a movie so well."

Sweet neighbor said, "Hey,
Here with us she could stay.
She could play here nearby
While our friends have game night."

So that's what they would do.
They left with sisters two,
And I played with this lady
Who I barely knew.

Her friends showed up and I played with them, too.

On this hot summer night
I felt mostly alright.
Their faces all shined
And the tile was bright.

I couldn't read,
So they read things to me,
But I didn't slip
When I showed off my splits.

Old lady said, "Hey,
It's a hot sweaty day,
And I'm feeling hungry.
Would you like some ice cream?"

When mom came to the door
I glanced down at the floor,
And I said with a blurt,
"I took off my shirt!"

Mom said, "You did what?"
With cross eyes and a huff.
Then she looked at sweet lady
To find out more stuff.

With her wide, glassy eyes
Neighbor smiled in reply,
"Well, you know it's July,
So I hope you don't mind."

Her old friends waved out the door in goodbye.

Momma said, "That's okay,
Such a hot summer day."
When I held Momma's hand,
We stepped onto the sand.

I asked Momma, "So,
Tell me how was the show?"
When she said it was fun,
I knew our day was done.

I climbed on the bunk
And my thoughts got to thunk.
I stared down at the floor,
And my shaky heart sunk.

I laid in the bed
With sad dreams in my head,
Wondering if little Bliss
Knew what show I had missed.

That night I knew sometimes I could hold still.

Bunk

I'm jumping, jumping on the bed.
I'm jumping, jumping on your head.
I'm jumping, jumping 'til you're dead.
I'm jumping, jumping on the bed.

Now Bliss was having a good time
When she was making up this rhyme,
For she was jumping on the bed,
And she was right above my head.

Kids have fun with rhymes and jumps.
They like the sounds of springs and thumps,
But when the bunk came crashing down,
She ran away without a sound.

Then mom came in to see my screams
And found my tears beneath the beams.
I sobbed in fright and hitched my breath
As I told her they'd planned my death.

This fear was just as real to me
As any threatening thing could be,
For Bliss and Plan, they liked to play
With ways to scare me every day.

My mom knew not what she should do
To find a way to make it through,
So she pushed past the sibling junk
And promised me the upper bunk.

Then anywhere bunkbeds were near
It brought back this life-threatening fear.
And so, I always got the top,
No matter who thought that should stop.

Bliss and Plan quit playing games,
Their teamwork crashed in guilt and shame.
Either of them had fun with me,
Though their alliance ceased to be.

Then Plan and I were doing fine,
And Bliss was always a good time.
With sisters three the group is odd,
And so I had to be the mod.

From that day on they fought and picked
At which of them had sharper wits.
They were afraid of what may come
If they should work together some.

For sibling rivalry is fine
And so few pay it any mind,
But no one wants their sister dead,
Even when jumping on her head.

Standing Tall

My dad is tall.
His arms are long.
He loves to sing
A hallowed song.
And every time
I need a rhyme,
He reaches down
To help me climb.

So he must be
A sturdy tree,
Who always stands
Where he should be.
He branches out
To have some fun
And slowly stretches
Toward the sun.

Whenever there's
A tree around,
The air is full
Of breezy sounds,
And everyone
Who's on the ground
Is looking up
Instead of down.

Fawn

So I live with the frog and bee,
The swishy fish and singing tree,
And they all love to call me near
And whisper wishes in my ear.

I walk around with wobbly knees.
With careful steps, I long to please.
And since their grievances I hear,
They think I'm just a tender deer.

This fawn is all they seem to see
When they lean in to speak to me.
What they don't know
Is deep below,
In me
There lives
A salty queen.

Squawk

One weekend we went to the Lake
To swim, sunbathe, and ride the waves.
I thought this trip would be so grand
Because of Papaw's birthday plans.

My grandpa is a baseball fan.
He watches every game he can.
For his birthday we brought a gift.
I knew he'd love to open it.

We were all together in a room.
He would open our gift soon,
And I just couldn't wait too long.
I had to see his smile come on.

My grandpa, though, he likes to talk.
He hunts for stories he can squawk.
So sometimes I think he's a hawk,
Though this would cause some minds to balk.

He picked our present up, and then
Touched the paper briefly, when
A story popped into his head
And all my patience soon was dead.

He started his story.
It must be more boring
Than seeing his smile
Shine brightly a while.
I burst, "Oh, shut up and open it!"

Everyone laughed.
He smiled and nodded.
He opened the present
And we all applauded.

But mom pulled me aside, and she was so mad.
She said I had really behaved so, so bad.
She said, "You do not get to say that.
You listen.
You don't get to squawk over him,
Not one minute.
So I want you now to go see your Papaw,
And tell him you're sorry for your rude guffaw."

I was so upset.
I was so embarrassed,
Did not want to disappoint
My perfect parents.

So later that day,
On a walk by the Lake,
I told Papaw Hawk I had made a mistake.
I said, "I'm so sorry."
I felt terribly bad,
And the hot tears I cried
Were so terribly sad.

He said, "That's okay, now
You did nothing wrong.
It doesn't hurt me
To hear you sing your song.
I know what you meant.
I know why you did it.
So give me a hug,
You're already forgiven."
And that was the day,

For the first time I think,
When I thought sometimes
I could do more than just listen.

Dissed

One day my sister Bliss
Was feeling very dissed.
She'd been talking to Plan
And didn't understand.
She wanted to be cool
With all Plan's friends from school,
But Plan didn't agree,
Since Bliss is just a bee.

I told Bliss it's okay,
She could still play her way.
If Plan didn't want her
It wasn't such a bur.
Someday she'd get to know
What she could really show,
And play with bees like she,
And buzz between the trees.

But Bliss didn't agree.
She wanted to be seen,
Though Plan didn't want her
To buzz in her water.
Bliss tried to fly along,
The current going strong,
And when Plan swam away,
It ruined Bliss's day.

Trip

I had a gifted teacher who
Was way more than super cool.
Mrs. Leap was really neat.
For weekly classes we would meet.
She fed us thoughts our minds gobbled
And we flocked near, a bit warbled.
The subjects taught were so distinct.
She really helped us learn to think.

One day she took us out of town
To see a play that moved around
About a boy who flew away
And found a land where he could stay.
He never had to listen to
Grown-ups or any well-to-dos,
And every day
He could be
Anything he wanted to.
I thought that would be so grand.
Never did I in my land
Wander free or fly away
Or feel like I could save the day.
And that boy looked so, so brave
Each time he flew across the stage.

When the show was over though,
On a bus we rode back home.
I talked to my turkey hen,
And she told me a secret then.

She said,
"That boy was actually
Played by a woman acting free.
Her back was hurting terribly.
But she wanted to act so badly,
She never thought of losing track,
And played her part,
Despite attacks
From awful aches
That would come back
Each time she lifted
Off the stage."

I spent the ride back home thinking
About one small, important thing:
That boy or girl or in-between,
Who danced and flew and fought and sang,
Had not shown one sign of pain.

The Shadow Dance

A shadow taps along behind
Because it doesn't have a mind.
It shuffles back
Along a track
That bends away when spotlights shine.

Now Plan, she was the brightest star.
Her smile beamed from near to far,
And we all knew
That it was true,
Her sparkling eyes could stop a heart.

And me, my hopes are just a dream,
From heel to toe my steps unseen.
They look through me,
"How cute is she?
Trailing this flashy beauty queen."

Great beauties need a shadow there
To echo back their every care,
So people see
When they should be
Applauding that bright glow they share.

And everyone will dance along
To music she is playing strong.
They sing her praise,
Their cameras raised,
When all I want is my own song.

Ups and Downs

My mom
Is hopping
Up and down.

She gets
So mad
When there's a sound
That can't be good
Or can't be down
Or can't be hushed up
All around.

She jumps on Plan.
She jumps on Bliss.
She jumps on Dad.
She jumps on this.
We know she needs
To find a log
And sit awhile
In the fog.

But she knows she's
A clever frog,
And doesn't want
To be ignored.
She thinks she would
Feel too left out
Upon a log
And being bored.

So any time
She gets like this,
We try a bit
To then insist
She take a break,
And take a breath,
So she doesn't
Just hop to death.

Biting

One day I wandered by the stream.
My sister Plan swam up to me.
She knew there was a bigger place
Where she could dive and leap and race.
She said she'd met this creature who
Thought it would be oh so cool
If she would swim along with him.
He knew a way to the ocean.
It sounded like a good idea.
She really didn't fit right here.
I thought his smile seemed too sharp,
And told her he might be a shark.
She said, "I don't care what you think.
I feel like I live in a sink!
And I don't want to wait right here
Beside a wibbly wobbly deer."

And so she left with him that day,
And found some harder games to play.
Eventually back home she came.
It ate some part of her away.

Stacking Up

I guess I'm just a tender fawn.
I like to wander through the lawn.
The frog and tree,
Big fish and bee,
Are creatures all of which I see.

So with the busy bee I play,
Leap with the fish when she's my way,
Sit with the frog beside the pond,
Talk to the tree about his fronds.

There are some troubles brewing, though.
The fish is just too big, you know,
And she thinks it would be so grand,
If she could find some bigger land.
So she keeps leaping for the trees
When really she should swim to sea.

The frog is looking for a log
And trying to stay clear of dogs.
And with her big and bright round eyes,
She's sizing up the tree's tall height.

This tree she is hopping around
Is standing there without a sound.
And since he likes to sing in town,
He's often seen with a small frown.

The bee to every flower dives,
And cannot seem to find her hive.

She likes to fly around the frog
But shouldn't be stuck on a log.

And they all ask me what I think,
But they think my advice just stinks.
As each of them keeps whispering,
Each small wish keeps blistering.

Every day there's problems new.
Every worry stacks up, too.
It's true this land is packed
with stacks that smack
of creatures
screaming soon.

Buff

I was small a long time ago,
And my favorite animal
Was a buffalo.
I'm not sure why.
They're such big size,
With horns
And hooves
And big dark eyes.
But if I could get close enough,
They looked so soft
And full of thought.

In middle school,
Mr. Leap
Sent everyone
In quick retreat.
He seemed immense
And bold and wise.
His presence filled
A giant size,
And most kids thought
He was so gruff.
But I thought
More thoughtful stuff,
And he did one of the greatest things
That ever helped me find my wings.
So when I look at stories to show,
He's my favorite buffalo.

He brought poetry
To me.
Then wanted a chance to see
What all our poet skills
Could be.
He read my
Lonely Thoughts
To himself.
Then he read them
Out loud
To everyone else.
He was so proud
That I had found
A thing to say
So profound.
His smile shined.
His eyes were kind,
And he said I could blow some minds.

I said, "You're a wise buffalo,
But what you don't seem to know
Is everyone around here
Treats me like I'm just some deer."

He said,
"There's a place you can go
To find a brighter way to glow,
A summer camp for gifted kids."

So that's exactly what I did.
And Summerscape
Was really great.
New parts of me came wide awake.

Before the camp
Reached an end,
I met Iris,

A special friend
Who said, "My dear,
To see your bling,
All you need is polishing."
What I had to do to shine
Was get to know
What's really mine.

Light

I sit alone
in a cold, dark
and lonely place
every tiny noise
screams out at me
from the void
of the moment
then
a tiny spark ignites
suddenly
faces appear
warm, happy faces
filled with empathy
and love
I look down
and find
the light
is coming
from
me

Platform

Mr. Eagle's class at Summerscape
Was all about the risks we take,
When standing up or standing out,
Or learning what to do without.
So often times we'd take a trip
And talk about group leadership,
To get outside our comfort zones,
In search of other skills to hone.

One day he took us to a yard,
And this new test was really hard.
We searched within for trust in all
As we climbed up to lean and fall
Back into arms stretched waiting there,
If we could override our fear.
So one by one, we fell on back,
And everything was right on track.

When on the ground, I'd cheer for who
Had climbed up on the platform to
Fall back into our waiting arms.
We knew we'd catch them without harm.
It was quite an honor though,
To stand there waiting, and to know
The one up there was trusting you
To make your promise follow through.

My turn upon the platform came
And suddenly this was no game.
Though clearly I could hear them cheer,

I could not ignore my fear.
I almost didn't take that risk,
This vital lesson almost missed:
When arms are there stretched out for you,
Don't let fear tell you what to do.

You let it wash across your heart,
But don't turn back from where you start.
And there will be a tipping point,
Where everything within you joins,
And all you feel is one great rush,
And all your doubts are quickly hushed,
And anything is possible
Beyond all limits you had known.

Adrenaline floods through your skin.
You just want to do this again,
When nothing brittle holds you back
From giving without any slack
And shining brighter than the sun,
Shouting in front of everyone,
That we are here to live and die,
And all you have to do is try!

'Cause we are here to breathe and be
The fullest incarnation we
Can find within our minds and show
The world the greatest truths we know.
So don't you take a step away
From what you have to do or say.
For life is one fantastic stage,
But you decide what's on your page.

Eagle

Reaching out
Grasping hope
Conquering fear
Soaring high above the clouds
Afraid of nothing
But possibilities
Taking our minds
And creating
One soul
One heart
Laughing and crying
Singing and dancing
Praying and hoping
Trusting strangers
Putting your life in their hands
Being reborn as a perfect whole
Feeling pure love and excitement
Accomplishing the impossible

True

Mr. Eagle
Sat next to me
And said, "What would you like to be,
If you had one power
Beyond belief
And had to choose
Between these two:
Would you like to fly high above
Or be invisible to everyone?"

"To fly," I said without much thought,
That answer was easy enough.
He said, "Then you're an extrovert."
I laughed so hard, and out I blurted,
"That's not true, for I can see
An introvert is what fits me."

"No," he said, "This quiz tells you
Which is which that's true for you.
An introvert prefers to hide.
An extrovert prefers to fly."

But can you see?
My answer was plausible.
I'm plenty familiar
With feeling invisible.
But if I could soar through something blue,
Then I could feel something new.

Unconditionally

Go out on the ledge
Jump off
Head first
Dive
Into a dream
Make something
From reality

A frightful night
Recreates pandemonium
Don't be scared of shadows
Friends appear where you least expect them
Throw yourself into selflessness
Take a risk
Accept yourself
Love someone
Unconditionally

Carrier

It was my junior year of high school.
I was sure I'd be so cool.
Summer had been really keen.
I felt like I could be a queen.

And there was a guy named Jesse
I had been trying to somehow see.
But he was hard to nail down.
I never could find him around.

So after a few weeks and a day,
My dear friend Misty came my way,
And what she knew could cheer me up:
A different guy did have a crush.

Now Misty is a friendly girl
Who likes to spread around the word
Of what's been what and who's been where
And where's been why and how's been there.
She likes to be where people are,
And sings her songs both near and far,
Chirps about with messages
In all of her expressiveness.
She lights up my day start to end.
She's my favorite pigeon friend.

I said, "Who has a crush on me?
She said, "This boy named Brett, you see."
I asked, "How does he know me, though?
I've never seen him at this show.

I don't know anyone named Brett.
I think that's a name I wouldn't forget."
She said,
"I'll introduce you two.
Meet me later after school."

His flashy smile was fast and free.
And he seemed to like looking at me,
But I had never seen his face.
I wasn't sure about this place.

I said, "I don't really know
Whether I should point my glow.
I don't know who you really are.
You only know me from afar.
So let's spend a few days or a week,
Getting to know the speech we speak.
And we'll be friends a little while
Before I really show a smile."

That was the day I met Brett,
And I was right.
It's a name I wouldn't forget.

Wondering

Wonder why
I want to cry
Each time I crack a smile
Wonder why
I want to fly
Each time I sing a song
Wonder why
I want to die
Each time my heart begs please
Wonder who
Can get me through
My deepest, darkest fears
Wonder who
Will stay true
With me all my years
Wonder who
Can open eyes
Accepting all my flaws
Wonder who
Can lend their heart
To all who have a cause

Shiny

Brett said, "I'm in this Writers Club.
I think you would like to come.
It's usually a good show.
There could be people there you know."

And I did want to go.
I'd heard of it long ago.
That little nudge was just enough
For me to think I'd show my stuff.

So the next day right after school,
I was feeling really cool,
And walked with Brett up to the room
That flipped around my afternoon.

For there he is
My Mystery Man.
Can steal wild hearts
With a single glance.

"Jesse Teller!" I exude.
"I have been looking all over for you."

"Well, I'm right here," he responded soon,
His smile so shiny to light up the moon.

"Yes, you are," I hungrily said
While picturing tastiness inside my head.

I swayed 'cross the room,
Sat close as I could,
And twinkled my smile
To show we were good.

He started the group.
I'm not sure what they read.
I flirted and grinned,
Forgot all about Brett.

I was really nervous
About giving a read,
But I promised Jesse
A poem next week.

I left that room flying high in the sky,
And shining so hard I thought I might die.
All I thought then was that life would be grand.
I had no idea about Brett's fishy plans.

Glow

Plunge into an inner consciousness
Vaster than the open spaces
Left within their hearts
Original and distinct
Love like never before
Feel your heart overflow
Into the lives of those in need
An openness characterizes
Your face, your smile, your glow
The enchanting glance
Of a warm summer night
Forever dwelling in your soul
Peaceful sighs for days to come
Happiness to be left alone
Faces seem to erase the past
Of promises meant to last
Risk it all
In exchange for everything
Be you
And no one else

Bait

Brett called me,
I talked to him.
Said, "Let's get to know you then.
Where do you like to go?
Who do you really know?"

He said
His very best friend
Was this guy named
Jesse Teller.

"Really?" I said,
Pretty stoked in my head.
I had to get close
To this guy he knew most.

"Yeah, where Jesse is, I'm always there,
Plus my best friend, his name's Glare.
We all hang out every day,
Every night and everywhere."

"I really want to see those places,
Be around a certain face, and
Maybe you could let me know
Next time you go to their show."

"Sure I can," he said to me.
"But they're a tight group, you see.
So first I'll need to talk to them,
Let them decide if you are in."

That made some bit of sense to me,
And I really wanted to see Jesse.
So I waited a few days or a week
For Brett to make another speech.

Desperation

Every minute
With you
Escapes
Before I can catch it
Every thought
Of you
Disappears
Before I can say it
Every place
Without you
Is a nightmare
Of lonely faces
Every dream
About you
Wakes me up
Before I can live it
Every emotion
I feel for you
Astonishes me
Until I believe it
Every time
I see you
My heart smiles
Before you can see it
But not before you can feel it.

Misdirection

I thought this day
Would be so great.
I had some tasty
Risks to take.

I spent all day
Trying to play
With what exactly
I would say.

I had a friend read
Static
Just to see if I
Could hack it.
She loved it,
So I planned to go
To Writers Club
And show my stuff.

Brett met me at
My locker then
Right after school
Had reached an end,
And did something
I did not see,
Something somewhat
Cruel to me.
He asked me not to go that day,
Not to come to show and play,
Said Writers Club

Was his one thing.
He didn't have
Many things to thing,
And how could he
Keep up with me
If I thinged my things
Plus one to be?

I actually did feel bad for him,
And a little mad,
but then,
He bent his eye,
And frowned just right,
And begged me not
To be uptight.

So I huffed.
I'd had enough.
There's somewhere else to show my stuff.

At the time,
I didn't know,
Brett had just hijacked my glow.

Static

53

I've got bumblebees flying into my ears
And I'm running in place toward the wind.
It blows dirt in my eyes.

Dandelions frolic across the dried grass
And the birds in the sky try to dance,
But the radio's broke.

Wildfire glides by the sparkling lake
And my life seems to echo away,
But it says the wrong words.

Touch
The world's
Dark core
As your heart screams,
Smile. Quiet, my dear.

Look,
Don't touch,
They all seem to say.
And the eyes in the back of my head
Watch my dreams walk away.

A Lonely Charade

They see her smile.

She camouflages a neurotic emotion
Guilt, pain, depressed by the expected
How to escape?
Wanting something surprisingly close
Too far to grasp
Wisdom failed to warn her

Cheated out of something
Something she didn't want
Until she had it
But it's gone
Everything slips away without warning
At war with herself, inside she cries

They see her smile.

Illusion

I kept asking Brett when
I could hang out with
His friends.
I tried
To find a way
To spend
Some time
With them because
Of that one guy,
And Brett kept saying,
"Don't be rude.
I'm a cool dude.
They need time
To decide
If they want you
In their group."

Finally he said,
"Just chill out.
It can't be you
I talk about
Every time I see them,
Every day I meet them."

I kindly tried not to whine.
He said, "Something else to try,
These tournaments with
Magic cards
They play sometimes
Without regard

To who shows up
So anyone
Could join a game
To have some fun."

And if I won,
It'd be so grand,
They'd surely want me
In their land.

"Do you know this card game, though?" he asked.
Magic, I did not know.
So kindly Brett offered to me
To help buy cards and gladly teach
The rules and tricks of all of it,
So I could catch this ball,
Of which I'd been chasing around so long:
Time with this group
That sounded strong.
Brett said so much
They valued him,
He'd be the one
To get me in.

How Good

So how good do I have to be?
I'm waiting here trying to see
How long it takes
For me to make it
In with this
Tight group of his.

Brett said he'd help me
Play this game
And every weekend
He explains
How this card works,
How that takes skills,
How this deck's built,
How that spell kills.
And all this time,
In my mind
I'm proving I'm
The coolest kind
Of person who would
Do the most for
This impressive group.

So how good do I have to be?
And Brett, he just keeps testing me
To see if I can win
When playing him
Who's quite
The one to beat.
It's been a few weeks and a day.

So many of these games we've played,
And now I beat him more and more.
He has to let me in this door.

We finally show up at this show
And see who's there I want to know,
To join up in a
Magic game,
With who all's
Gathering this day,
And play and play.
Though no one's there
But little Scruff
And Brett's friend Glare.
When I win,
They seem surprised.
They stare at me
With blown up eyes.
I impressed them all,
No doubt.
By then I couldn't figure out
Why I felt so let down,
This win
Felt like
A loss
Somehow.

Switch

Eventually I asked Brett out
After he explained about
The group having this one rule:
Girlfriends were always cool.

I knew in that group I'd belong.
Everywhere else felt so wrong.

I thought I'd find just what I wanted,
Spend less time feeling so haunted.
It turned into the opposite.
It was like Brett flipped a switch.

He wanted his friends all to him,
Said I shouldn't hang with them
Because I'd be around too much.
His life was his and such and such.

He had his friends and I had mine,
And we could not spend all our time
Together between everyone.
Some time apart would be more fun.

That made a little sense to me,
Some things live
Independently,
And that turned into
Lots of days
Of arguing
About the ways

I couldn't tag along with him
Any time he saw his friends.
And bit by bit,
Blow by blow,
My little light
Lost its glow.

And somehow
No one seemed to know.

Stay Alive

The rain trickles down,
The sun burns our feet.
Laughter cries of yesterdays
That words would not repeat.

Time creates the future,
We create the past.
Hope restores the memories,
Tomorrows seem so vast.

Birds echo through
The trees singing songs of joy.
Timeless beauty will return
To lost souls once destroyed.

Clouds stare down across the land
And scream into our minds.
Hearts will smile at themselves
Since love makes them so blind.

Darkness cloaks the morning sun,
Stifling every breath.
Chills dance upon your spine,
Rejoice approaching death.

Happiness is lost in space
Upon the memory of your face,
Frightened by the realms of grace
Believing in your soul.

Love will stay alive.
Hope will disappear.
Close your eyes and calm yourself
As the end draws near.

Making Peace

The peacemaker she called me.
She said it with a sigh.
She meant it as a compliment.
I think I'd rather die.

I'll tell you what it's like
To be the one who makes the peace.
I'm always on the job here.
I never feel relief.

And if I'm the one making peace,
Then war is all my fault.
When battle rages it must mean
I somehow dropped the ball.

I have to fight to understand,
Each day, each week, each year,
The growing tension brewing
Through the pain and anger here.

I have to solve the problems
Of a world that makes no sense,
To soothe each wounded heart
And hear their grievance and defense.

And if it's something I can't fix,
Or don't know how to see,
I fail them all because they know
The peacemaker is me.

The weight of it is stifling.
The pressure is unfair.
But no one notices until
The peacemaker's not there.

So I could never leave my post,
Never wander free.
Their unbalanced relations
Can't reside here without me.

Peace is hard to make here
And I'll never understand
How it came to be my job
To sit with them and hold their hands.

To study every nuance,
Every glance and every glare,
Then after every battle
Comfort each one injured there.

Everywhere I look
There is a conflict they can't see,
And in my head, I picture
The work just ahead of me.

Explosions and collapses
Decimate supporting beams.
There's so much pain to witness
In the wrath and tears and screams.

And in the midst of battle,
Insults flying through the air,
I sort through all the bullets
Because I'm the one who cares.

I need to understand this war.
I need it all to stop.

I need to hurry up and
Make more peace before I drop.

Can anybody else here
Learn to work a bandage, please?
It's really pretty simple.
I can show you what you need.

It's just that all this peacemaking
Has worn me pretty thin.
And if no one here will help me
Then the war is what will win.

I think having one peacemaker
Is a terrible mistake.
I need you all to see
There is a point at which I break.

And the making peace, it kills me.
It's a dirty, thankless role
In a land with no compassion
For the empathy I hold.

I think maybe this position
Shouldn't be a job for me,
And that understanding conflict
Is for all of you to see.

Because my heart is breaking,
And I long to wander free,
And I know I'll fail you all
If all you want from me is peace.

Courtly

He bows
then takes
her tender hand
to dance
a song
the night demands
they turn
and nod
and slowly sway
their courtly
ways are
on display

For she's
the queen
of homecoming
her night
began
with golden rings
her hair
is swept
in curls and pins
her dress
shines bright
with crystal trim

His hair
is boldly
drifting down
his mane

and shoulders
frame his crown
he takes
you in
no questions asked
for he's
the king
of all outcasts

And kings
know lords
and ladies stare
allies
or enemies
are there
so they
hold tight
their loyalties
when mixing
with the
royalties

How
he moves
is art and grace
to dance
between
each focused gaze
and guard
the ways
of his dark land
as he
turns through
their powdered hands

My realm's
filled with

insanity
my bells
and whistles
wander free
my wardrobe
is a
travesty
and no
one knows
my pedigree

Woe
for me
i'll never find
a touch
with power
so divine
but i'll
pretend
i dance with him
and won't
collapse
before this ends

Demands

After months of emptiness
I finally got away from Brett.
I tried to find what I wanted
But nothing fun would get started.
I tried and tried to date a bit,
But no one would agree to it.

I'm not sure why
I can't get a guy.
Each one I ask
Throws me in the trash.
What's wrong with me?
What do they see
That turns them away
Every day?

Mom says,
"There's nothing wrong with you.
It's them. The guys, there are so few
who really can appreciate
All that you initiate.
You need someone smarter
Who won't have a harder
Time keeping up with you.
You're going to college soon.
Maybe you'll meet someone new."

"But that's not what I want," I say.
"I want someone here, today,
Someone who knows this town,

Who's lived here and been around
Long enough to see its glow,
Long enough to really know
There's something special happening here
Something magic in the air."

"Well, what else do you want?" she says.
"What list sits there in your head?"

"I want someone who'll dance with me,
Someone smart and funny,
Someone creative who can be
The gentleman I surely need,
Who knows what really matters most,
And feels like home, and holds me close.
Someone who's loved me far and long,
Someone who can hear my song."

"Wow," she says, "that's quite a list.
It's simply too much to persist.
I think you should rethink your plans
And come up with fewer demands.
No one can be all those things.
So think of what guys really bring,
And look for someone who gets close,
Maybe who can fit the most.
But let go of that lengthy list.
No one like that exists."

What You Don't Want

When I was a senior in high school,
I wasn't sure if I was cool.
It had been months since I broke up with Brett.
I hadn't really bounced back from it yet.

For so many days,
In so many ways,
He helped my self-esteem slowly degrade,
And convinced me the people I wanted to see
Saw nothing interesting about me.

When Senior Prom
Started coming along,
I watched all my friends
Making plans that were strong.
And everyone had a plus one
For the show.
Everyone knew
With which who they would go.

Pretty soon the question
On everyone's list was,
"Who are you going
To Prom with?"

"I don't have a date,
But it's really okay.
I always have fun
At dances anyway."

"Oh, that's not cool.
Do you want some help?
You don't want to go
To Prom by yourself."

I was really okay.
School was nearly all done.
I could have one more dance,
One last night of my fun.
No date would ever dance wild with me,
To spin and sway like their spirit was free.
So I was okay with going alone,
But everyone else
Thought that was all wrong.

Brett walked up with his flashy smile
And said, "Can we talk for a while?
Would you like to go to Prom with me?
It would be a good time."

But I didn't agree.
"No," I said.
"I'm through with you, Brett."

"Come on," he pressed.
"We could go as just friends."

Ugh, I huffed,
It was never enough with this guy.
Hearing no
Wasn't part of his flow.
After I finally said
I would think about it,
He left.

I was so done with Brett.
He had never made sense,

All his time keeping me
Separate from his friends,
And with them was always
Where he chose to be.
When dances came up,
He never went with me.
So why prom?
Why now?

Then my sister Bliss said,
"I'm here to help.
You don't want to go
To Prom by yourself.
So who's on your list?
If you could pick anyone,
Who would you choose
If you got what you wanted?"

"Well, actually," I said,
"There's one guy on my list,
Jesse Teller,
I like him quite a bit."

"Really?" she said.
"I know he is cool,
But he's already out of high school.
I don't think he'd go.
You don't really know him.
The chances of him saying yes are slim.
You want a date
Who means something to you,
Someone you knew more of
During high school.
I think you should go with Brett.
He is a date you could certainly get.
But whatever you do,
Whatever you felt,

You don't want to go
To Prom by yourself."

There was only one guy I wanted to kiss.
There was really no other man on my list.
So I asked Jesse Teller.
I was nervous a bit,
And this would be tricky business.
He was no longer in school.
Graduated last year,
And he wasn't a fool,
But he hadn't moved on,
Hadn't gotten away,
And his friends, lots of them,
Wanted him to just stay,
Not to leave or to change
Or to grow or to be
Anything different
Than what fit their needs.
But he wasn't very happy.

So when I said,
"I'm going to prom,
But it won't just be me.
There will be lots of cool people to see.
Some friends of yours
Are friends of mine.
You could come with us
And have a good time.
I think it'd be great
If you could be my date."
He didn't actually hear what I said.
He heard something else instead.
Something like,
You spend too much time with your friends.
All this playing around needs to end.
It's time you grow up.

It's time you should see,
Life can't be made out of fantasy.
There was a change in his eye
When I saw him decide,
Something about himself,
Something about me,
Something about his
Destiny.

"I can't come along.
I think you'll be fine.
Go with your friends.
You'll have a good time."

So I drove away
with rain on my face,
Knowing one day
I'd get out of this place.

My friend Misty said,
"Are you going with Brett?"

"I don't know, I guess.
Jesse didn't say yes."

"That's too bad," she said.
"I know it's not swell,
But you don't want to go
To Prom by yourself."

So I said yes to Brett
And we had a good time,
But all night I knew
Something wasn't quite right.

Then the next day he called me,
And the next after that.

He told everyone
He had won me back.
I was actually the last one he told,
But you know,
Hearing no wasn't part of his flow.

And I'm sure the next year
Would have gone differently
If someone had said,
"Listen to me.
It's possible
you'll only hear this once, but
You
Are the one
Who knows
What you don't want."

Blind

Starving my heart
Helpless against the cruelty of the world
Wondering about everything
Nothing matters
Fearful of the life ahead
Scornfully seeking relief
Timeless feelings
Mixed up in my soul
Innocence demented
Love twisted
Weeping through games
Laced with reality
Confiding in myself
Afraid to speak the truth
War rages in my soul
Confusion invades ecstasy
Happiness is lost in emotions
Expectations cease
Contentment lies
In every minute
Together
Without him
I am lost
With him
I am me.

Death and Taxes

I was eighteen
When I lost my dad.
He didn't pass away,
He just killed us.

I used to talk to him
About his work.
He used to explain things
I thought I'd need to know.

See, he was an accountant
For the geological survey,
And before that,
he worked on maps,
And before that,
He sold insurance,
And before that,
He sold jewelry,
And before that,
He built furniture,
And before that,
He sold shoes.

So I thought he knew a lot
About how things worked.
I would ask him questions
And listen.

One day he said he was having an accountant do last year's
taxes.

"Aren't you an accountant?" I asked.

"Well, yes," he said.
"But last year some things were different
With the house
And your mom's piano students
And some other things.
So it's just easier
If I pay someone else.
Tax codes change.
There's a lot to keep track of."

I'll be honest.
I hadn't thought much
About tax codes.
So I asked him,
"Should I use an accountant
When I'm on my own,
When I'm doing taxes?
Is that the way to go?"

"Well," he said. "it depends
On what kind of job you have,
What kind of income,
But you don't really need to worry about that,
Because probably, what will happen,
Is your husband will take care of those things."

In that moment
I had only one certainty:
I could not listen to him
Anymore.

You Never Know

One day Mom sat across from me.
She was feeling buzzy.
She said,
"I've been talking to Brett,
And you probably don't know this yet,
But he really wants to marry you."

"Yeah, I know.
He talks about it a lot."

"Well,
He's afraid
You don't want to marry him,
That you think he's not good enough
To be a Lynch.
And he's afraid you don't
Take him seriously,
But he really loves you,
And that's what you should see.
So what do you think
Of this scene you're in,
Tell me,
Why wouldn't you marry him?"

"Well for starters,
He hasn't asked me.
He just talks about it
All the time,
When we're going to get married,
When we're going to get married,

But he never asked me.
He's planning our whole life
And I never had a choice."

"Maybe he hasn't asked you
Because he thinks you'll say no.
So tell me now,
Is that how it would go?"

"I don't know.
I'm just not ready to get married.
I feel like something's missing,
Like something's not quite right.
I'm not sure if he's the one.
We don't get along that well,
And he doesn't want me around his friends."

"Well,
He feels like you wouldn't accept them,
Like you wouldn't
Accept him.
You know, there have been lots of times
When I really felt like
I wasn't good enough
To be a Lynch.
But your dad loved me anyway,
And if he hadn't,
You wouldn't be here today.
If he had listened to anyone else,
We wouldn't be together.
And I know we haven't always been happy,
But we have each other.
No one is perfect.
You have to accept people for who they are,
And love them truly
In spite of their flaws.
Your dad's love

Made a huge difference to me,
So just think about it,
Please,
Because we're so happy we have you three.
We love you girls so much.
So you never know
How things will turn out.
You never know.
You never know.
You never know."

Freedom

One weekend we went to the Lake
To swim, sunbathe, and ride the waves,
But this was the Fourth of July,
So there'd be fireworks tonight.

I always wondered how
Fireworks are so loud.
They never say, "Excuse me."
Or "Sorry for the fuse length."
Or "Would you mind?"
Or "Could I please?"
Or "Is it too weird
How I breathe?"

Fireworks just soar on up,
Then burst apart
As they erupt
And shine so bright,
So hot and light,
For all the faces near who might
Long for beauty in their sight.

Every heart is bathed in peace.
Every soul here wants to breathe,
To bask in power they create
When showing up
To celebrate
The future of the land
When freedom is at hand.

The Cliff

There's a cliff
Downtown,
And I know that doesn't make sense,
So you'll just have to listen
While I try to tell this.

It's high above a creek,
And it's not hard to find.
You just have to know
Where to turn right.

It's out in the open
Where anyone can see,
But everyone is moving fast
For where they want to be.

When you look across the valley
There's an old highway,
Weathered there through many years
For people who don't stay.

And if you creep up to the edge,
Look down, there's a spring.
On a hot clear day
You can hear people swimming.

Deep below that spring
Lies an uncharted cave,
A cavern so expansive
It's an unsuspecting grave.

So put yourself right there
Upon my rocky cliff,
And see it in your mind
While I tell you this.

I can see the highway
Across the valley deep,
And I can hear the laughter
Near the bubbly creek,

But I can't seem to get there
From this ancient cliff.
I can't find the parts of life
That I sit here and miss.

There's nowhere to go from here
As I stand on this ridge.
There's no cliff on the other side.
I'll never find a bridge.

And I cannot count all the times
I've longed to fly away.
If I could leap far enough,
Would I have to stay?

Or could I be part of this scene
That's right in front of me?
To soar beyond the grave and stream
Across this deep valley?

I can't see a way from here
To reach the other side.
As far as I can tell,
Upon this cliff is where I die.

It's all right here in front of me,
A vast expanse of beauty.
No path through it I can see,
So from this ledge, should I leap,
And see if I can fly,
Or what it's like to die?

'Cause I can't live here on this cliff.
There's not a water source.
There's no shelter, no nourishment.
There's nothing but remorse.

If I could just step off this ledge.
I'm standing right upon the edge,
And all I need
Is one small leap,
As I imagine in my head
Soaring free across this land
To reach that old highway,
And fly all night
To find a life
Where I would want to stay.

So what exactly would I lose?
How much would I regret
If I could summon up the strength
To take a single step?

The Infinite Pit

Emptiness
Tearing away freedom
Crumbling hope
Erasing dreams
Fires burning hateful flames
Leaving ashes
Nothing more
Eating time
Hungering
Taking all
Asking for none
Stealing the light
Hurling into a slow
Deepening, infinite pit
Unsure of where it ends
Or if it ever does

Breaking

Keep it together,
Just keep it together,
You have to get home
Through this inclement weather.
I can't see the road,
And the fate of my soul
Is gripped tight,
Knuckles white,
Through this unsafe unknown.
I can't stay with him,
I just can't let Brett win
When his blatant attack
Pushed me back.
Fading thin
Through his slippery games
Didn't come without strain,
But his grip makes me sick
And I can't let this slip.
This right here is the line.
There is never a time
When a snap, smacking back,
In hot wrath should be fine.
I can't fake a grin.
I can't deal with this sin,
But don't ask me to stand in a room next to him.

The very next day
I would put on the brakes.
So I told him to meet me out in the driveway.
Then I said, "We are through.
I want nothing to do with this future
Where everyone chained me to you."

He wept in regret.
He wished I would forget
His big loss of control
That left me defenseless.
He wanted not to see
The hate he brought to me
And he cried in reply,
"But we're supposed to get married."

Everything froze
And my clarity rose.
In this moment I saw it
So clear in the road.
I could point to his hate
And finally make him say
What the source of his rage was that got in our way.
So I asked him to see
What he felt about me.
Then he said it out loud
In a bout of relief:

"I hate you because you're always right!
I hate you because you're so good at everything you do.
There's nothing I can do better than you.
Do you have any idea what that's like to live with?
It's impossible!"

I'm not sure what that did to you,
If you could feel what I went through.
At least someone finally said
What they all hid inside their heads.
And now, my greatest mystery solved,
Why everyone was so appalled
When they spent too much time with me
Or acted like I shouldn't breathe.

But I cannot give any less
Than what I know to be my best,
So there's no way for me to live
When this world hates what I can give.
And I don't want to make you hate,
Yourself or me, make no mistake.
I'd rather cut off both my arms
Than inspire any harm.

I'll have to slink away in bed,
That's where I belong instead.
I don't even want to be dead,
Just leave me alone in my head.
'Cause no one wants to see me shine,
And no one wants to be mine.
My life is all a waste of time.
I can't pretend like I'll be fine.

Something Borrowed

I feel so lost.
It's dark in here.
Everything
Is full of fear.
I can't even
Find my heart,
And I don't know
Where to start.

Jesse leans in
Across the way,
Sees I need
Some help today.
He offers a hand
Out for me,
Glows a bit
To help me see.

Pulls me out
Across a bridge,
On wobbly knees
And shaky limbs,
Says, "Just stay here
A little while,
It's okay if
You can't smile.
I see your land
Looks pretty dark,
And I won't tell you
Where to start.

Lay here with me
Now and dream.
I've been searching
For a queen.
Lean in close
So you can see
What you think
Your dream would be.
Take your time,
Your mind is fine.
I'll hold you near
Until you shine.
If you need light,
Just borrow mine.
Your thoughts are not
A waste of time."

His glow is warm.
It feels like home.
And with his light,
I find my own.

These Two

He has these two friends Burg and Bell,
And they both get along so well.
Their friendship means more than you know.
It's clear in what they both will show.

Now Burg, he is a big, big guy,
Thick in the chest and shoulders wide.
He wraps his mitts around your head,
And hugs so tight you might be dead.
His roar is clear to all around
Whenever he decides to sound it off
To ones who scoff or cough
At those who make his heart feel soft.
He seems just like a bear to me,
But ferrets are his favorite kind
When animals are on his mind.

Well his friend Bell, he loves bears
Though
He's slim and sleek
and not so slow.
His reflexes and wits are quick.
His paws are thin
Instead of thick.
Bell likes to play where people are
And darts around town in his car.
He's very cool
With everyone,
Knows lots of ways of having fun.

So Burg the Bear
Prefers ferrets,
Though Bell's the one
To really wear it.
But he likes bears
And keeps Burg there
Because these two
Make quite a pair.

a tiny seed

It's Sunday morning, rise and shine,
We've got worship to do.
Pick out a dress and curl your hair
To learn why God loves you.

Hallelujah, sing along,
Let's praise Him every week.
We know He loves the strong.
We know He loves the meek.

Sit here and listen, quiet now,
We want good girls and boys.
If you're too jumpy or too loud
You won't hear my voice.

I listen to the service.
I hope I'm being good.
There's lots of life ahead of me
And I do what I should.

Today's speaker is a guest.
His message here is new.
The lesson is the love of God
Is unconditional and true.

He loves us when we're broken.
He loves us when we're sad.
He loves us when we have no choice
But to suffer something bad.

He knows we can't be perfect.
He knows we can't be pure.
And anytime we need Him,
He's there to reassure.

I've never known a love like that.
I don't think it is real.
It sounds like myth and mystery,
Something I can't feel.

Inside me there is so much pain
That I don't understand.
I seek the comfort of God's love
Throughout this lonely land.

I know God loves the strong.
I know God loves the meek.
But my spirit is broken.
I know my heart is weak.

Every day is empty.
Every face is clean.
The world just blurs right past me,
My suffering unseen.

And if God loves the broken,
And if God loves the sad,
Then why is my heart empty?
Why do I feel so bad?

I cannot comprehend a love
That's unconditional.
It must be myth and mystery
From verses of the Bible.

Myth and mystery it is,
But I just can't let go

Of the tiny seed it planted
That really wants to grow.

Tiny as a mustard seed
Buried in doubt and fear,
The bit of hope that one day soon
I'll know that God is near.

Days and weeks blow past me.
This hope just won't let go.
But nowhere near, inside or out,
Does God's love seem to show.

I stay up late, I weep and moan,
My lover comforts me.
But we know he is broken, too,
And light is hard to see.

He tells me of his suffering,
He tells me of his pain,
And every time he talks to me,
He feels a little sane.

So one dark night he tells me
Of a time he hates to show,
A day he broke the broken,
A rage I've never known.

And though I know I love him,
And want to hold his hand,
This violence, harsh and senseless,
I cannot understand.

In wrath and fear he says to me,
"I've lived a horrible life.
You can't judge me for what I did
While trying to survive."

Then out the door he runs away,
Off into the night,
So lonely, dark and desolate.
And this empty room is quiet.

My heart, my hope, my future,
Everything is still.
And in this bleak, unlikely place
I can hear God's will.

This one, he is so broken.
This one, he is so sad.
And in his life, he's had no choice
But to suffer days so bad.

This one needs to know
A love that's unconditional.
And wherever this road leads,
Loving him will teach it to me.

I'm not sure where I'm going.
I don't know what's ahead.
And this small seed inside of me,
I thought it was dead.

A tiny sliver opens,
And out from it can grow
A love so deep, so vast and strong
That I have longed to know.

So be still and listen,
And put away the noise.
If you're too jumpy or too loud
You will not hear His voice.

He knows we can't be perfect.
He knows we can't be pure.
And in your darkest, bleakest times,
He's there to reassure.

For God does love the broken.
He loves the souls in need.
And He can change your empty life
With just a tiny seed.

Clever

"Look, deer, I'm a clever frog.
Just because I need a log
Doesn't mean I don't know
Which way you should point your glow.
If you would just listen to me,
I can tell you what to see.
Look closer at how he treats you.
Someday soon I think he'll eat you."

"There are some things you don't know.
You don't get to point my glow.
He's the reason I still shine.
When I'm with him I feel divine."

It wouldn't hurt

It wouldn't hurt…
It wouldn't hurt…
It wouldn't hurt to say,
Each time you say it wouldn't hurt, you redirect my day.
Each time you say it wouldn't hurt, you rip my choice away.
You scold me to be careful as you tell me what to give.
You scold me to be grateful as you tell me where to live.

If you would…
If you would only…
If you would only let me be.
The person who I am is someone you can't seem to see.
The person who I am is different than you can believe.
If you would only look and listen to the words I say.
If you would only let go of this need to save my day.

Why won't you…
Why won't you just…
Why won't you understand?
I don't need you to tell me what I want or what I am.
I don't need you to tell me what to love about a man.
If I won't marry someone soon, then I'll just be alone?
Well, I can think of things far worse than being on my own.

Dear To Me

We flew upon the Dragon Wing
Over Six Flags and everything.
We played and giggled through the day,
Napped and soared in every way.

We swam between the people, then
Slid past a row of sands, and when
I looked up through the wave I saw
A stream of color there.

Some longing deep and dear to me
Hitched close and wondered what could be,
But all I saw
Were shadowed walls,
So I ignored her timeless plea.

"What's that?" he asked.
"You want this here?"

"No, it's okay.
I'm just a deer."

He said, "it sounds like mystery,
But you are so much more to me.
Stay here,
Just stand here and breathe.
Do what you can
To finally be
The sacred beauty I can see."

He touched my hair
And kissed my crown,
That's when I knew
His queen was found.

So I gazed out
Across the sands,
All colors here at my command.
I tuned with the key of their song,
Echoed from wells deep and strong,
And one by one,
As they asked,
I conjured a bottle
Of sand and glass.

I lifted it and held it close,
Just like the one I love the most.
He smiled and said, "We're here all day.
Are there any more you want to make?"

But I knew our greatest feat was done.
So I replied
With open eyes,
"All I need is
One."

Warm

One week he took me to Wisconsin
To see the city he grew up in.
He showed me all around the town
And told me stories all about
Things he'd done and things he'd do,
And lively people he once knew.
Then we dressed up and went to see
Some of the people he mentioned to me.
They were having a big party
To celebrate an anniversary,
And all night long
We danced and played,
And everything felt okay.
His cousins then up to me came,
Their names Tigress, Lioness, and Grace.
Now I'm not very good with names,
But this time wouldn't be the same.
They said, "We're going to play a song,
And maybe you could come along,
And dance and sing and laugh with us,
If you think you can gaff with us."

"I simply live to dance and sing.
It makes me feel just like a queen.
And everything feels really sane,
So I would love to play this game!"

They thought it was really cool
That I would jump into their pool.
Honestly I felt so free,
Their glow as warm as light could be.

Oversight

My grandma was wise.
She had big bright eyes,
And she had a grasp of immeasurable size.

So, much like an owl,
She'd fluff up her cowl,
And get a reaction with only a scowl.

She surveyed her land
When making a stand,
And dove into problems that needed a hand.

I loved her so,
But what I didn't know,
One day her ignorance started to show.

She pulled me aside,
Said, "Don't be his bride.
There's bipolar problems on both family sides.
And if you're with him,
When you have children,
This mental disorder might show up in them."

I was horrified.
Some part of me died.
I was actually too offended to cry.

How did she not see
The mistake that would be?
I asked, "How can you say that to me?

If that gauge was in place
When my parents had babes,
I wouldn't be standing here today.
If our kids are bipolar,
We'll bring to them order,
And know how to teach them about their disorder.
So don't you tell me
How my life should be
When this trepidation is all you can see."

Finally

"Before you go, I want to ask you something."

"Okay, what?"

"Well, I've noticed
when you come home on the weekends,
you stay at his apartment."

"Yes, I'm 19 years old. I can do that."

"Well, don't you need to sleep in your bed?"

"I sleep just fine at his place."

"Well, you're not coming to church with us on Sundays.
Is he not letting you go to church?"

"It's nothing like that. I'm just busy all week
and I want to sleep in.
He's not 'making' me do anything, mom.
He's not like that at all.
I'm happy for once in my life.
I'm finally truly happy.
Why can't you be happy for me?"

"I'm just worried about you."

She's crying now,
She's trembling.
The louder I get,
The deeper the crease on her forehead.

The house is dark
And I'm leaving.

                              "Stop worrying about me.
                    You don't need to worry about me."

"I'm just worried you'll get hurt."

                              "He's not going to hurt me."

"You can't know that.
How can you know that?"

                              "Because he's not capable of it!"

"Why would you say that?"

                              "Because he understands love!
                                        He listens to me
                    And he wants to know what I think
                              And he loves me in ways
                                        You never have!"

                              Slam the door and I'm free.
                    That's not a conversation she wants to finish.
                              There's nothing else she can do.
                    If she wants to kick me out, that's fine.
                              I know where my home is now.
                                        I'm finally safe,
                                        I'm finally free,
                    And I hope she kicks me out.

Enough

I thought kicking me out was the worst she could do,
And honestly I was prepared for it, too.

It wasn't enough that he loved me.
It wasn't enough that we were happy.
It wasn't enough that he filled up my list
Of everything I'd ever wanted to kiss.
It wasn't enough that I finally felt free.
It wasn't enough that he understood me.
It wasn't enough that we had agreed
To the dress she picked out
Or the church she had found.
It wasn't enough that our date was set.
It wasn't enough that our parents had met.
It wasn't enough that he'd bought me a ring.
It wasn't enough that I was nineteen.

Nothing they saw was ever enough.
I had not gone to their church in months.
I told Mom I felt the divine when outside,
And experienced God other ways in my mind.
When I was fourteen Mr. Eagle had said,
"Your daughter's beliefs have changed quite a bit.
I hope that won't cause problems at home
Because her understanding of life is her own."
It wasn't enough that Mom's therapist
Had said, "Whenever you're feeling upset,
Don't try to fix someone else.
Look at what's happening inside yourself."
It wasn't enough that the same therapist—

When seeing me too—said, "Nothing's amiss
When you decide what's important to you,
And live your life by your best rules.
Everyone has different beliefs
And we all have the right to privacy."

None of it was enough.
You'll see.

They came in and sat down,
Frowned a bit and looked around.
They brought into our sacred space
A load of sins that filled the place
With wrath and pride,
Judgment, and hate,
Even their own envy or greed.
She said we shouldn't move in together,
Told him he was corrupting her daughter.
Then I knew
My life was cursed.
My spirit had never felt worse.
That was the night my future died.
Everything inside me cried.
I was locked
Deep in a cage,
And no one knew
I needed saved.
No one here
Could break me free
From their strict sensibilities.
I curled up tight.
I sobbed and cried.
They never paused
Their homicide,
For they ended my hope in life,
Gutted me just like a knife
Had cut through all my purest dreams

And pushed me down
Under their feet.
Then they said, "Let's pray for you
Because that's what we want to do."

And they prayed to the Lord their God
Who wept with me
And my only love.

They finally left,
I'm not sure how.
Nothing seemed to matter now.
They ambushed our way of life,
Proving it wasn't ours to decide.

But Jesse, he's the best of us.
He said to me, "This is still up to us.
If you could choose anything,
What decisions would you bring?"

I cried,
"Everything
Is going too fast!
I don't know how
I can last
When all this pressure
Is never gone
And every week
Is hard and long.
I just want to live with you,
To take our time
And find what's true,
And push the wedding back a bit,
But none of that matters to them.
How can we get them to see,
What's important here
Is what matters to me?"

And honestly,
Neither of us knew
How to solve this issue.
But after a few uncertain months,
How I felt about him
Wasn't enough.

Too Much

"Jesse broke up with me.
For good.
He's seeing another girl."

"Oh deer, what happened?"

"Are you kidding?
Everything I said would happen did.
You can't do all that to someone's heart.
You can't make two people get married
before they're ready.
He's been hurt too much.
He can't stand to be around me.
Now he's just trying to move on."

"Well that's not my fault.
I'm not in charge of his decisions.
If he can't stick around
that's his problem."

"This is not his fault.
I'm going to beg him to still be friends,
and if I'm lucky,
he'll consider it."

Apologies

Emotions take you where you dread going
When led by your heart
You find yourself in desperate situations
Why do I feel like everything I say is wrong?
I don't mean to hurt you
But I do
Circumstances go beyond my control
I didn't want to hurt you
How could I?
But I did
It shreds my heart
To see you suffer
You're the spark that gets me through each day
At the edge of giving up
I think of you
And find renewed strength
How could I have been so stupid?
I need to protect you
But I failed
And caused you grief
And pain
I'm sorry
The guilt may never disappear
I pray I'll never hurt you again
But I'm afraid I will

Prey

They say if you just find your light
And let it shine, you'll be alright,
But little lights are vulnerable
When stepping out in wind that blows.

And no one thinks about the flame
That tries to glow out in the rain,
Or what it's like to shine too bright
Around creatures who stalk at night.

The phone rang and I answered it.
He said, "Hey, it's me Brett.
I heard plans were called off with Jesse,
And you still mean a lot to me.
There's a few things I regret,
And if you're not over me yet,
Maybe you could buzz me in
And we could try to start again?"

I said, "No.
I won't forget
The things you said or did that kept
Me feeling so upset or small.
I don't want you in here at all."

He said, "Listen, you can't sympathize
Because you can't look in my eyes.
I'm here to apologize.
You know you overanalyze.
Let me come up to your room.

I want to see you smile soon.
I'm just here to check on you
And find out what else we can do."

"I am not buzzing you in,"
I abruptly said to him.

"Okay then, fine.
Just let me see you,
Say sorry,
And leave you be, so
Come down here to this front door
And talk to me out on this porch."

"Fine," I sighed.
And went outside,
Drying off the tears I cried.

I saw him then
Across from me,
Showing a disarming lean.
His eyes were soft.
His ears were keen.
He tried so hard to seem serene.
He said,
"You know,
When we broke up,
My mom was so down on her luck.
She screamed at me for days and days,
Because if she could have her way,
She really wanted us to work.
She loved you and called me a jerk."

"She screamed at you?"

"Oh yeah, you see,
She wanted us to get married."

"Well that's not ever happening,
So you let go of that old dream."

He asked, "Is there anything I can do
To try to make it up to you?"

But I'd heard his chatter before,
And I needed to slam this door.
I couldn't trust this sneaky voice
That would devour all my choice.
I recognized the hungry grin,
The quiver underneath his chin,
A truth I would not soon forget,
To see when Brett was desperate.
I saw the danger in his lean,
In this apparently shy scene,
The shine behind his
Eyes obscene,
A smile that flashed
Beguiling dreams,
The reason for his
Charms a scheme,
This hyena cleverly hunting.

I had to be careful here,
Not to let him any nearer,
So I chose my words with care,
Hoping anger wouldn't flare.

"I want you
To go far away.
Go somewhere else
And find a way
To be happy
Away from me.
That's where I want you to be."

And that was just enough for him
To pack away his flashy grin,
To stifle his unnerving cackles,
To leave without raising his hackles.

Flame

When the whole world is against you
And no one's on your side
Your heart gets tired of fighting back
And the flame will slowly die
When no one understands you
Or what you love and why
All reasoning diminishes
And gradually stupefies
When everything you've worked for
Suddenly burns itself
You wonder how you could be right
Confidence hides on a shelf
The one thing that was always good
Is suddenly so wrong
They tell you he won't understand
Your future isn't strong
Loved ones stab you in the back
Their shallowness exposed
You're left confused and wrinkled up
In a world that's not your own
A lonely, tired, angry world
You're better off alone
But that's what everyone else believes
You waste your life at home
Happiness a distant memory
An unforetold mistake
Each day withers miserably
Your heart forgets to break
The love they thought would tear you down
Was truly meant to be

Your frightened, empty, hateful heart
Just should've been let free

Consequences

If people would truly listen
If only they would believe
If everyone would trust us
They wouldn't feel deceived

If love was taken seriously
If pain did not exist
If strangers didn't care
Perhaps they wouldn't persist

If happiness was forever
If justice conquered doubt
If parents believed their children
They'd understand what it's about

If I had to live without you
If love never knew my name
If your voice never trickled into my heart
I'd surely go insane

Normal

"You've been living with him a few months now.
It's time you talk about getting married."

> "Are you kidding?
> After the way things went last time,
> I'm never saying the word
> wedding
> to that man ever again."

"Bekah, this isn't right.
It's not healthy.
It's not normal."

> "I don't care what's normal!
> I'm exactly where I want to be.
> I'll live with him the rest of my life
> and never get married
> if that's what he wants to do."

"But Bekah, what about your kids?
If you aren't married,
that's so hard on the kids.
They need a stable home life."

> "We might not have kids."

"What?
Why wouldn't you have kids?
How could you not have kids?"

"I don't know if I want to have kids.
I don't know what kind of parent I would be.
I certainly can't think about that right now."

Reprieve

I called Grandma Owl and asked if she would come see me.
The past few months I had been living with my dear Jesse,
And we'd been fighting every day against his family.
It had blown up on our front lawn just the prior week.

Now it was his birthday and we had to celebrate,
To find a way to make his day a bit elaborate.
His mom had called expecting all to be just like before,
And he hung up on her because he was so rightly sore.

So Grandma Owl came to town to take us out to eat.
In after her came Papaw Hawk, looking rather beat.
We chirped a bit with them inside our home on
    Normal Street,
Then headed out the door to find a night of sweet reprieve.

I pulled aside my grandma and said, "Thanks for coming
    down.
I know it's quite a drive for you to come from out of town.
I need tonight to go well, so certain topics are off.
How did you present this trip convincing Papaw Hawk?"

She said, "I told him, 'Honey, I know what you think
    of him.
But I'll tell you something that I've noticed about them,
Bekah's only happy when Jesse is around.
It's not our job to understand the happiness she's found.'"

And for one night in late March of 2001,
I thought finally all our battles would be done.

That night of peace was way too brief and it just
    wouldn't last,
In spite of all the darkness we had fought through in
    our past.

125

Solo

I hung up the phone
And I said, "That was Job.
I have to go talk to Jesse a moment."

Mom was enraged.
She took center stage
And said, "Don't you go talk to him today!"

"He just wants my key
And a minute to see
If I'm done moving out of Normal Street."

"This is a trick!
You don't want to do this.
You can drop off the key at a leasing office."

She didn't know
This wasn't her show,
Or what I'd been trying to work out through Job.

I knew she was wrong,
But I had to go on,
And at this point I hit a false note in my song.

"He just wants the key.
I don't care what you see!
He's made it clear that he doesn't want me!
I am going," I said,
My heart filled with dread.
I had to sort through all the notes in my head.

We had taken a blow,
Lost all faith and all hope,
And somehow he blamed me, for what I don't know.

But each time I tried
To make sense of his eyes,
I'd crumple within all the tears I would cry.

Determined to do this
Without being a nuisance,
I said, "I'll pretend to have laryngitis."

But she was determined
To push through her sermon
Without letting me get another soft word in.

Then she surmised
With a glare in her eyes,
"If you're that upset, then you should let your Dad drive."

"That's fine," I sighed.
"I don't want to drive,"
Afraid at the thought of the tears I might cry.

So Dad drove me to see
My ex-lover Jesse
At the shell of our home on Normal Street.

I walked up to him,
And his face had a grin,
And he didn't look mad,
And he didn't look thin.
He looked light and free.
How could it be
That he was so happy
And I was so... me?

I wrote down my lines
And stared in his eyes.
His face in that moment I have memorized.

Somehow I was to blame.
I felt so ashamed.
These past days without me had made him
        look sane.

    Then I walked away,
    'Cause I wanted him safe,
    And thought living without me was his
        saving grace.

But the world made no sense.
My future hopeless,
The next week I went to a new therapist.

I said, "There's something wrong with me.
I'm here to find out what it is.
        Every time I care about someone,
        It drives them to total madness.
            I can't figure out what I'm doing,
            But I want to be able to love.
                This problem with me keeps
                    happening.
                It's one I just can't solve."

    We spent the first hour
    On a form we devoured.
    I answered his questions without feeling sour.

But what could I do?
When we were through, he said,
"I think there's nothing wrong with you.

Closure is what you need
To help you feel free,
So I want you to tell your story to me.

You can say anything.
We'll see what it brings
When someone listens to the song that you sing."

Plan

When Jesse told me he had DID,
Honestly I was so relieved.
When sorting through our history
It made it all make sense to me.

By then I knew I knew him well,
And all I wanted was to help.
He'd need support without conditions,
No expectations or traditions.

My relatives go by the dozens,
Word spreads through sisters and cousins,
So I had to make the calls
To explain this new plan to them all.

The hardest one was my big sis.
Plan didn't want a word of this.
She didn't care about my plan.
She didn't want to help this man.

"You keep letting him hurt you.
I don't know why you're staying true.
Walk away and get over him.
You deserve so much better than this."

To me that sounded ludicrous,
So I set fire to my script.

"What *I* deserve?
You are worried about what *I* deserve?

This is a man who has been through Hell.
He is a good man
And he is trapped there.
He is trying to find a way out of it,
And I can hold his hand.
I can help him through,
To show him there's a better life,
To show him he can live Heaven on Earth.
And if I can do that,
Then I should,
And I will,
And there is nothing you can say that will stop me."

And that worked,
Plan started to see.
For me, it was a small victory.

I couldn't turn anyone else around.
When the topic came up, they all sort of frowned.
And every time they frowned at me,
I was glad Jesse wasn't around to see.

There was so little I could do
To make them really see the truth,
But if I was able to give him a clean slate,
They could have set aside their hate.

The Bridge

In 2001
Everyone
Thought Jesse and I
Were done.

At year's end
Job, his old friend,
Said, "I've decided you don't know
Which way you should point your glow.
Just give up that old dream home.
You'll never repair these broken bones.
Imagine if you will
A bridge,
From him to you,
From you to him.
That bridge has taken too much strain,
Too many wounds and too much pain.
You can't restore
A bridge that's bore
So many blows
And so much more.
Just go build a bridge that's new,
With someone else who can be true."

This bridge idea is really old,
But Job feels like he's spitting gold.
And though it was a quiet night,
I didn't want him to be right.

The damage hadn't come from us,
And I hoped it could be enough,

If we took more time to explore
The deeper cracks our old bridge wore.

Bride To Be

My life was at a different stage
When I called my parents to say, "We're engaged."
Years had gone by filled with sadness and rage,
But finally our story had turned a new page.

I told them our plans for a wedding next fall.
Sometime next October we'd schedule it all.
"We're taking our time and we won't drop the ball."
Then I waited to see what they'd do with this call.

Their quiet reaction filled me with dread.
No way I could know all the thoughts in their head.
From all past examples, our plans would be shunned.
Then Dad said, "We'll buy a new dress if you want."

Some clouds rumbled in and it started to rain,
As my brow furrowed tight from old heartache and pain,
But I steeled my resolve in the wake of the stress,
And I said, "Oh no no, I'll be wearing the dress."

This dress was on clearance the day it was sold,
The style discontinued was what we were told.
Then after I thought all our love had run cold,
I had decided to do something bold.

I offered it to a consignment shop.
It hung on their rack while the prices all dropped.
But after six months it was still hanging there,
Evidently something no one wanted to wear.

This dress no one wanted, I hope you can see
How this dress was perfect for this bride-to-be.
It was only white satin, no sequins or beads.
The heart on its back was all it would need.

It waited so long for its day in the sun,
And now was its chance to show everyone
That no matter the damage their actions had done,
With patience and virtue his heart I had won.

For the rest of the year they let me plan the day,
Went along with the script that I wanted to say.
By then they all knew the last card they could play
Was just to stand back and stay out of my way.

The last night before our wedding scene,
I sat down with my party and told them my dream.
"The next day, just this once, pretend like I'm a queen.
Just humor me and you'll see what I mean."

I sat in a chair while they braided my hair.
If they tried to complain, I wouldn't care,
But my cousin Flower turned the tide for me.
With a smile she bowed and said, "Yes, Your Majesty."

Our Kingdom

One weekend we went to the Lake
For special vows we two would take.
Our flower bearer led the way,
And there weren't too many waves.

I gladly stand here as his queen.
My glowing king is next to me,
And in a gentle sacred breeze,
Our hearts join in sweet ecstasy.
From me to him,
From him to me,
We both know we're finally free.
Then we step out
To look about
The world that spreads beneath our feet.
And all the creatures in my land,
All of them can understand.
Today they see the bridge that's here
Between that wolf and their small deer.
The Frog and Tree,
Big Fish and Bee,
Flower, Ferret, Bear, even
The Owl and Tigress,
Hawk and Lioness,
Spider, Serpent, Pigeon friend,
Buffalo and Turkey Hen.
Everyone here still and bright,
Every light shining this night.
They dance and play
Within the scene,

And all night long
Feels like a dream.
They sing the melodies they seek,
And play out their own sweet beats.
I unwind
In kind
And find,
Here tonight,
In love and light,
All creatures in this sacred sight,
They feel alright.
They're shining bright.
And we delight
In this sweet night,
Our kingdom full of peace.

Post Script

There was no way to deny on that day
All the love that we had and the parts they had played.
So many battles had stood in my way,
So many lines they all thought they should say.

And for so many nights I wished long and hard
That just from the start they'd let us play our cards.
For all their opinions and judgment that grew,
Some wisdom was missing from what they all knew:

Sometimes you're the one who is leading the show,
And what's in your script are the truths that you know.
But then you step back and you sit in the wings,
Or you're part of the crowd and you learn different things.

I know my lines and I know my part,
My truth woven deep in the strings of my heart.
And isn't a role in which others would shine,
But it's perfect for those who are one of a kind.

ABOUT THE AUTHOR

Rebekah Teller grew up in the wild backwoods of southern
Missouri. Raised by crawdads and water gliders,
she became fascinated with language at an early age.
One day, while stumbling through a cave barefoot,
she rescued a lost storyteller, who ensnared her heart
and taught her to speak.

www.ingramcontent.com/pod-product-compliance
Lightning Source LLC
Chambersburg PA
CBHW050532160726

48003CB00002B/565